How to Read Scratch Computer Code

BY GEORGE ANTHONY KULZ

The Child's World®
childsworld.com

Published by The Child's World®
1980 Lookout Drive • Mankato, MN 56003-1705
800-599-READ • www.childsworld.com

Photographs ©: Shutterstock Images, cover (foreground), 3, 23;
Sabri Deniz Kizil/Shutterstock Images, cover (background); Wave
Break Media/Shutterstock Images, 5, 13; Scratch is developed
by the Lifelong Kindergarten Group at the MIT Media Lab. See
http://scratch.mit.edu, 7, 8, 9, 11, 15, 16, 18

ISBN 9781503823341
LCCN 2017944904

Printed in the United States of America
PA02360

ABOUT THE AUTHOR

George Anthony Kulz holds a Master's degree in computer engineering. He is a member of the Society of Children's Book Writers and Illustrators. He writes stories and nonfiction for children and adults.

Table of Contents

CHAPTER 1

What Is Scratch Code?

Nadine wants to make her own computer game. But she doesn't know how to make it. She needs to learn to write a computer **program**.

David likes to make animated stories. He wants to make one on the computer. He can do this through a computer program.

A computer program is a set of commands. They tell a computer what to do. They are written in a language the computer can understand. This language is called **code**. There are many types of codes. One of the most common computer codes is Scratch code.

You can make games and projects using computer code.

Scratch is a **visual** programming language. It is made up of building blocks, like Legos. The shapes, colors, and words inside each block tell you what each one does. When you put blocks together, you can make things happen on the computer screen. Creating projects, games, and art with Scratch is a snap!

CHAPTER 2

The Basics

Scratch has three main parts. These parts are the Stage, the Sprite List, and the Scripts Area. These parts all work together to help you make a program.

The Stage is where all the action takes place. Whatever happens on the Stage will happen on the screen. The Stage includes a backdrop. The backdrop is like scenery. You can choose a backdrop from the backdrop library. You click a green flag button to start your program. You click a red stop sign button to stop your program.

The Sprite List contains sprites. Sprites are characters or objects you can put on the Stage. Scratch comes with many sprites. One common sprite is called Scratch the Cat. You can also make your own sprite. Each sprite can have a costume. A costume is a different version of the same sprite. Each costume changes the sprite's position, or the way the sprite appears to be moving.

Cat1   Cat1 Flying   Cat2   Crab

Dinosaur1   Dinosaur2   Dinosaur3   Dog1

Sprites are like characters, or actors, on the Stage.

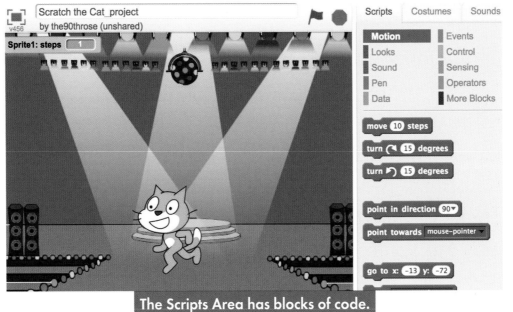

The Scripts Area has blocks of code.

The Scripts Area is where you write computer code. A script is made of blocks. The blocks are instructions. They tell your sprites what to do. Blocks allow you to control the action on the Stage. You can put blocks together to make a script.

SAMPLE SCRATCH PROJECT

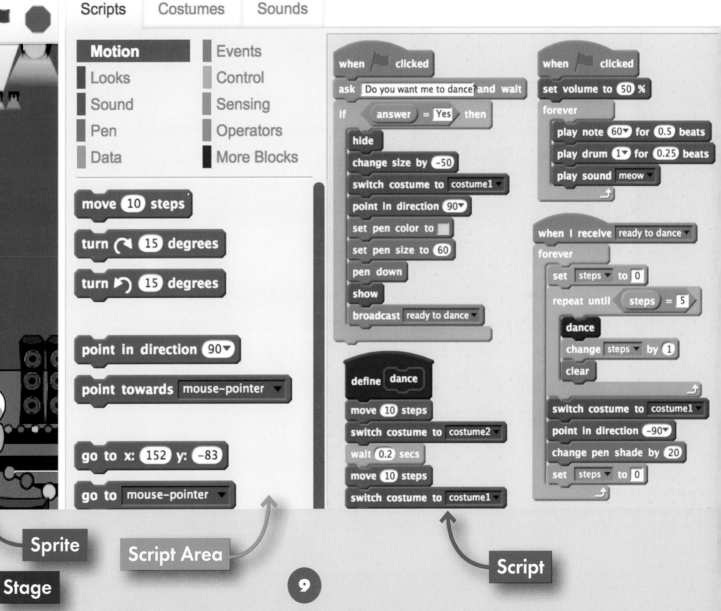

Scripts   Costumes   Sounds

Motion   Events
Looks   Control
Sound   Sensing
Pen   Operators
Data   More Blocks

move 10 steps

turn ↻ 15 degrees

turn ↺ 15 degrees

point in direction 90▼

point towards mouse-pointer ▼

go to x: 152 y: -83

go to mouse-pointer ▼

when 🚩 clicked
ask Do you want me to dance? and wait
if   answer = Yes   then
hide
change size by -50
switch costume to costume1▼
point in direction 90▼
set pen color to ☐
set pen size to 60
pen down
show
broadcast ready to dance ▼

define dance
move 10 steps
switch costume to costume2▼
wait 0.2 secs
move 10 steps
switch costume to costume1▼

when 🚩 clicked
set volume to 50 %
forever
play note 60▼ for 0.5 beats
play drum 1▼ for 0.25 beats
play sound meow ▼

when I receive ready to dance ▼
forever
set steps ▼ to 0
repeat until steps = 5
dance
change steps ▼ by 1
clear
switch costume to costume1▼
point in direction -90▼
change pen shade by 20
set steps ▼ to 0

Sprite

Script Area

Stage

Script

9

Using Blocks

Scratch's Scripts Area has many types of blocks. Different types of blocks are different colors. The color of a block shows what the block will do.

One type of block in the Scripts Area is a Pen block. Pen blocks are dark green. These blocks add colors behind the sprite. The "set pen color to" block allows you to choose the pen color. In the sample Scratch project on page 9, the pen color is set to yellow. Other Pen blocks change the pen size. Some erase all Pen colors on the Stage or start and stop drawing.

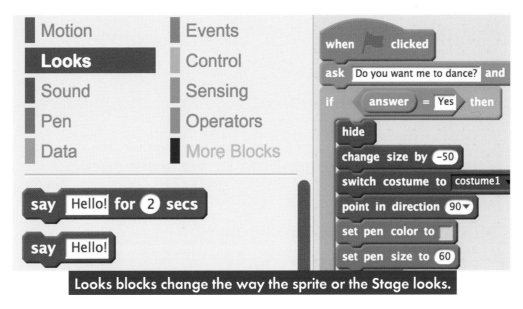

Looks blocks change the way the sprite or the Stage looks.

Looks blocks are purple. In the sample Scratch project, the "switch costume to costume1" block changes Scratch the Cat's costume. You can make your sprite appear to move by changing his costume. Other Looks blocks change backdrops. Some blocks make sprites think or say things using speech bubbles.

Motion blocks move sprites on the Stage. Motion blocks are dark blue. In the sample Scratch project, the "move 10 steps" block moves Scratch the Cat ten steps. Other Motion blocks allow you to turn your sprite or tell your sprite which direction to move. Another allows you to control how fast your sprite moves.

Sound blocks make sounds. Sound blocks are dark pink. In the sample Scratch project, the "play drum 1 for 0.25 beats" plays a drum sound for a quarter beat. Other Sound blocks change instruments, volume, or speed.

Behind the Scenes

Other kinds of blocks in the Scratch program make things happen behind the scenes. Behind-the-scenes blocks include Events, Control, Sensing, **Data**, and Operators blocks.

People who create programs in Scratch can use certain blocks to run commands behind the scenes.

Events blocks are dark orange. An event can happen when one part of the program broadcasts a message. Another part of the program does something when it receives the message. When the user clicks the green flag Events block in the sample Scratch project, the program runs the blocks that follow it. Another Events block in the sample project broadcasts the message "ready to dance." This message is sent to another Events block in a new set of code. The "when I receive ready to dance" Events block receives the message and runs the blocks that follow it.

Control blocks control when other blocks run. Control blocks are gold. In the sample Scratch project, the "wait 0.2 secs" block tells the program to wait 0.2 seconds before running the next block.

Some control blocks are statements that include "if" and "then." If a certain action happens, then this Control block runs the next blocks in the **sequence**.

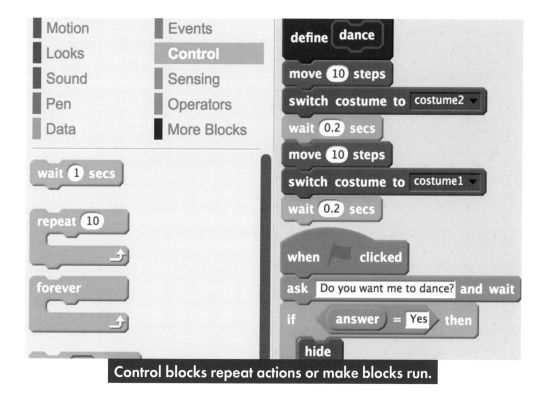

Control blocks repeat actions or make blocks run.

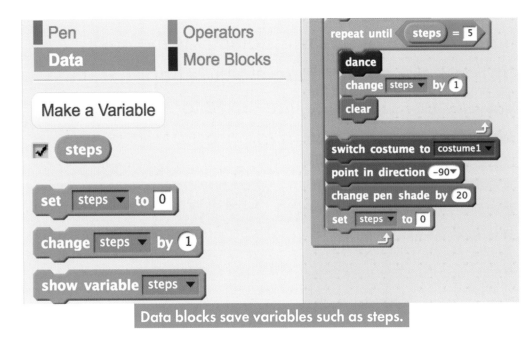

Data blocks save variables such as steps.

Data blocks are orange. Data blocks save data to use later. Data are invisible information that only the program can see. The program uses it to keep track of parts of the code that are important, such as **variables**. You can name your variables. A common variable is "steps."

In the sample scratch project, the "set steps to 0" block sets the value of the variable at "0." Under that block, a "steps" Data block along with a Control block tells the program to repeat the blocks that follow until the variable "steps" equals 5. The Data block "change steps by 1" adds 1 to the number of steps. When this set of blocks has been repeated until "steps" equals 5, the program moves on to the next part of the code. Since the repeated action involves dancing, this part of the code tells Scratch the Cat to dance five times.

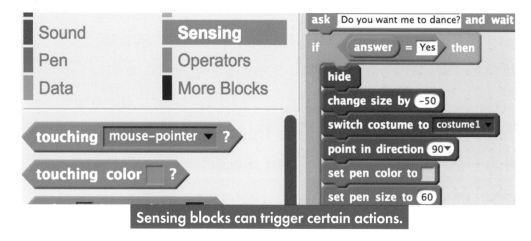

Sound	Sensing
Pen	Operators
Data	More Blocks

touching mouse-pointer ▼ ?

touching color ☐ ?

ask Do you want me to dance? and wait

if answer = Yes then

hide

change size by -50

switch costume to costume1 ▼

point in direction 90▼

set pen color to ☐

set pen size to 60

Sensing blocks can trigger certain actions.

Sensing blocks help the program **detect** things. Sensing blocks are light blue. In the sample Scratch project, the "ask Do you want me to dance? and wait" block will show Scratch the Cat asking this question in a speech bubble. The program will wait for an answer. The user can type the answer on a keyboard. Once the program gets an answer, it will run the next blocks in the sequence.

Finally, Operators blocks do things with data. Operators blocks are light green. They involve **equations**. Operators blocks can tell the program to add, divide, or subtract things. Another type of Operators block has an equals sign. In the sample Scratch project, the equals sign Operators block is combined with a Data block to make the "steps = 5" block. In this case, the Operators block defines the variable "steps" as equal to the number 5.

Now that you know how to read Scratch code, you can make all kinds of projects. It's time to get coding!

1. Where do you write computer code?

    A. The Stage

    B. The Sprite List

    C. The Scripts Area

2. What is the purpose of Data blocks?

3. Which blocks broadcast messages?

    A. Motion blocks

    B. Events blocks

    C. Sensing blocks

4. What is a costume?

GLOSSARY

code (KODE) Code is a language made up of words, letters, or symbols that a computer can understand. Scratch is a type of code.

data (DAY-tuh) Data are saved information that can be used later. The Scratch program can save data.

detect (di-TEKT) To detect is to discover or learn something. Sensing blocks in Scratch help the program detect things.

equations (ee-KWAY-shuhnz) Equations are mathematical statements that include an equals sign. Operators blocks in Scratch involve equations.

program (PROH-gram) A program is a set of commands that tell a computer what to do. You can make a computer program using Scratch code.

sequence (SEE-kwuhnss) A sequence is a group of things that follow a certain order. In a Scratch program, blocks run in a sequence.

variables (VAIR-ee-uh-buhlz) Variables are things that have values and that can be measured. Data blocks save variables in a Scratch program.

visual (VIZ-yoo-uhl) Something that is visual can be seen. Scratch is a visual programming language because the user can see it.

TO LEARN MORE

In the Library

Breen, Derek. *Creating Digital Animations: Animate Stories with Scratch!* Indianapolis, IN: John Wiley and Sons, 2016.

Wainewright, Max. *Code Your Own Games! 20 Games to Create with Scratch.* New York, NY: Sterling Children's Books, 2017.

Woodcock, Jon. *Coding with Scratch Workbook.* New York, NY: DK Publishing, 2015.

On the Web

Visit our Web site for links about how to read Scratch code:
childsworld.com/links

Note to Parents, Teachers, and Librarians: We routinely verify our Web links to make sure they are safe and active sites. So encourage your readers to check them out!

INDEX

ANSWER KEY

1. **Where do you write computer code?** C. The Scripts Area

2. **What is the purpose of Data blocks?** Data blocks save data, or information, for the program to use later.

3. **Which blocks broadcast messages?** B. Events blocks

4. **What is a costume?** A costume is a different version of the same sprite.